The Care Given and Forgiveness Withheld

Ori Sentiments

BookLeaf
Publishing

India | USA | UK

Presentation by *BookLeaf Publishing*

Web: www.bookleafpub.com

E-mail: info@bookleafpub.com

ISBN: 9789363310148

First edition 2024

Is This a Collection
of Poetry…

Or is it an excuse for me to
practice putting the busy thoughts
crowding my overactive mind into words,
because I always have
such a hard time doing so?

Is it a chance for me to ramble
without being interrupted
Without being dismissed,
argued with or talked over
Without being called overly dramatic,
an attention whore, a liar?
Is it a place for me to safely vent and
rant to my heart's content,
without fear of repercussion,
under a chosen name that
no one who has ever hurt me knows?

Or is it an outlet —
somewhere for me to go
with all the love I feel,
which is often too much for me to contain?
Is it a gasp of air gathered in
the sea of my empathy and appreciation

before I drown,
struggling under its waves
and the deeply ingrained belief
that I'll never be good enough
to deserve the love and understanding
returned to me?

I don't think I know how to write poems
I think I'm just trying to give a voice to
the drastic range of my emotional capabilities —
my silenced frustrations and overwhelming fears
and the hurt I'll always hold grudges over,
as well as all the gratitude and admiration and
adoration that I try,
but often fail to express in their entirety
to the people I care about

In 30 Years

My financial advisor is telling me
how much my investments will pay off.
Right now, it's very hard
for me to imagine still being around
to make use of that money.

I try to picture it, being fifty-three.
Do I have my life together by then?
Am I settled and secure and stable?
Am I happy?
My financial advisor believes
money can buy that happiness, but

do I read the morning paper,
sipping a cup of coffee that
no longer makes my heart race uncontrollably,
which was thoughtfully brewed for me
by someone who still can after so many years?
Are we living in a house with sturdy walls
that don't hold secrets and shame?
A house with creaky floors that I don't
carefully listen for sounds from?
Do I meet with friends
for brunch on weekends?
Was my relationship

with my mother and sister salvageable?
Is my father still alive?
How many dogs do I have and
what stupid nicknames have I given them?
Do I introduce myself to people
with my real name
and show them a version of myself
that isn't watered down for their comfort?
Am I embracing the new wrinkles and
stretch marks on my body?
Am I at home in my skin?
Am I still learning lessons and
growing because of them?
Did I ever go back to school and
do I have my dream job?
Am I helping others?
Am I the reason someone else is considering
what their life might look like in the future,
finding themselves
hopeful that things will get better?

Bookmarked Memories

"Someday, when I'm dead,
you'll tell your kids that I used to say this,"
you remark,
only after you said something funny, or
encouraging, or loving
"Someday, you'll tell them
that we used to do this together."
You say this over
weekly waffles and art projects,
whenever I'm smiling
and it's like you're trying to convince me
to remember you that way
by bookmarking positive memories
for me to reference when you're gone

But I'm not having children
and it's because the things
I know I'll remember most about you
are all the times you
started arguments with me just to see me cry,
then told me to stop being such a sensitive bitch
and sent me away to my room
to regulate my emotions alone

[Dear Dad,]

I'll think of all the times you talked down to me
and made me feel stupid,
like in fourth grade, when I was sobbing
over math homework I didn't understand,
while you got frustrated with explaining it
again and again, the same exact way
And now, you still make me feel like
I'll never be a capable adult and
won't survive on my own

Remember when I asked to take out a loan
to go to college with?
I wanted to go to a school far away from home
and live on campus to gain independence
(an ounce of freedom)
You didn't let me
You watched me stress over making deadlines
and online college payments
with my part-time, minimum wage job
and then bragged to family about
how I was working to
pay my way through school all on my own
(like I had a choice)
You were so proud of me
for graduating debt-free
with a degree I'll never use
I'm still not allowed to own a credit card

because the radio personality
you listen to religiously
says they're evil
I can't imagine how difficult it will be for me
to borrow money for a house
without any credit whatsoever
Your name is on my joint bank account
and I've typed,
"How to identify financial abuse"
into my Google search bar too many times

I'll remember when you got angry and
nearly beat my mother's favorite dog to death
When, in your rage,
you almost strangled this dog
You would have if Mom wasn't
screaming and crying for you
to stop and calm down

I'll remember all the times
you were misogynistic
towards the mother of your children,
asking her what was for dinner
after she came home exhausted
from her third job
The times you body-shamed her
while being twice her weight
That time you didn't defend her
when another man called her a terrible wife

I'll remember the many times you told
my little sister and I to cover up
because the tank top and shorts we wore
in the summer heat made you uncomfortable
I still can't wear shorts without
feeling unsafe from objectification in my body
I'll remember how many women you blamed
and how many vile men you've defended
while "playing devil's advocate"
Do you remember ranting
to your twelve year old child
about how marital rape doesn't exist?
Was I supposed to see you
the same way after that?
(I don't.)
Was I supposed to view your
relationship with Mom the same way?
Was I supposed to grow up having
healthy feelings towards marriage and sex?

I'll remember all the times you used
your religion to justify your hatred,
all the secrets I had to keep from you, and
how terrified I was that you would find them out
because I knew exactly how you would react
I knew I wouldn't be met with
the understanding and support
I spent my entire life longing for;
I would be lucky if I was *only* kicked out

You threatened to put me on the street over
something as small as the deck of tarot cards
that you found while snooping in my room

No matter what, you were never, ever wrong

I'll remember the stories you told me
about how you came to faith,
when you got drunk and
planned to kill your first cheating wife
and the fireman she slept with,
but didn't, because your best friend,
who had no memory of the night,
stopped you
and you were convinced that he was
actually an angel intervening
I'll think of the stripper you confessed to dating
and the motorcycle gang you joined,
how fatherhood wasn't enough
for you to give up drinking
In fact, I know these stories only because
you become so loose-lipped when you're drunk

[Dear Mom,]

God, your voice was so
grating and abrasive when you screamed,
which was almost every minute of the day
I'll remember that everything about you

was so loud and harsh,
even before you started going deaf

I'll remember how it seemed like
no matter what I did,
I could never do enough,
could never be good enough for you
I tried so hard to make you care,
but your narcissism had a funny way of
making me easy to ignore
and easier to dismiss
Maybe that's the privilege of being
your eldest child,
because you always liked
the younger one a little more
and chose to give her more
of your time and attention
(Why was that? I wanted your love too)
I'll remember how you pitted your daughters
against each other
and taught me jealousy and envy
(What does she have that I never did?)
After starting an argument between us,
you pretended our fighting broke your heart

I'll remember how you took a page
out of Dad's book and never apologized
You spun every single way you hurt me
into a situation where *you* were

somehow victimized by *a child*
You screamed at me, but
when I screamed back to defend myself,
you'd cry because I was yelling at you
You manipulated me into thinking
I was *always* breaking your heart
and disappointing you
You guilted me into
accepting the role of villain and
forgiving you every time,
despite you never once being grown enough
to ask for my forgiveness

I'll remember how I never had privacy —
no locks on my doors and no journals left unread
I never had a place to hide
from your critical eyes
A mother should try to build her children up,
but you tore me down
just like you tore yourself down,
because I was nothing but a reflection of you
I exist as a horrible reminder
of what you ruined your body for
You taught me to starve myself for
approval I never got

I'll remember how I spent my childhood
being your therapist
I heard every problem you had with your family,

a friend, or your husband
I took your side and was there to comfort you
every damn time
(Where were you when *I* needed
someone to listen to me, comfort me?
How did I end up being more of a mother to you
than you ever were to me?)

I'll remember how much you hated affection
All I wanted was to be held by you,
but now, I think, even if you did hug me,
it would feel stiff, forced, unnatural —
nothing like comfort or warmth
or like coming home
the way I imagined it'd be when I was a kid
I wanted to hear kind words from you,
but I think you were allergic to them
unless you were talking about yourself

Help

I look my mother straight in the eye
and tell her I want to be dead.
It's a cry for help, for comfort.
It's a plea to be seen
and to have my pain be acknowledged.

She meets my red-rimmed, empty eyes,
but does not see me.
She is too busy proselytizing guilt
when she says, "Then get right with god
so I don't have to worry
about where you end up."

There's No Love
Quite Like Christian Hate

Love the sinner, but hate the sin.
That's why I have to point out that
you're living so deep in it
that you can't tell which way is up
and which way is down.
That's why I must tell you that
you're walking the path to Hell.
You know, accountability and all…
You're being deceived and misguided
by the Devil.
He's leading you to a place
you'll never be able to return from.
God hates faggots and trannies.
(God hates *you*,
and I love you *so* much that *I* need to be the one
to drill this into your head.)
You're going to Hell!
Hell is not a metaphor
and you should be terrified.
Fear God. Fear His wrath.
Fear what He will sentence you to
on Judgement Day.
Repent. Repent. Repent
or God is going to turn you away and

disown you
(like your mortal parents should have).
You're going to burn forever in His absence,
craving Him, empty and full of regret
as you're tormented for all eternity.
Then you'll see that I was right all along!
(A wager of gold against your soul
says I'm better than you
because I believe and you don't.)
Have you even read the Bible?
(Okay, but have you read it *my* way?)
That's why you suffer —
you don't have enough faith.
If you were a better Christian,
if you prayed more,
that wouldn't have happened to you.
Beg for forgiveness for
those evil, impure thoughts.
Your mind is contaminated;
you have been corrupted.
(Don't touch me.)
Your body is a temple that has been defiled.
You are unclean, dirty, filthy…
You have given up your highest calling
and rejected the greatest blessing God
could possibly bestow on a woman.
What? Of course you're a woman,
(you Jezebel spirit!
I mean,) *my sister in Christ.*

Are you arrogant enough to think
you know yourself better than God does?
Who are *you* to rewrite His plans for you?
You need a strong man to submit to,
someone who can correct that attitude of yours
and cure you of your diseases.
(Then again, you don't deserve a man
if you can't give him children and sex.)
Lost little sheep, let me (be a hero and)
guide you back to the flock.
Come back; return to church.
I love you, but if you don't come back to God,
you can't be in my life anymore.
I can't have you influencing my children.
They can't see you acting happy without God,
(That's all it is, right? An act?)
or else they might think someone can actually be
happy giving into their
human nature and living in sin.
(They might think it's okay to be…
Like *you*.
Stay away.
You're poison.)
I love you, but (I'll laugh
when I look down from Heaven
and see you in Hell
because) I *tried* to warn you.
(You deserve worse.)
I love you, (but no, I don't.)

The Curse

You know,
the one passed down generationally
from my mother,
who inherited it from her mother,
who inherited it from the mother of all mothers,
Eve, who was set up by her maker to fall

The one I received like a debt
simply for being born as I was,
given to me over a test I never took,
but somehow failed,
over fruit I never ate, wisdom I never gained,
and a rule I never was given the chance to break,
yet still had to be punished for

I laugh loudly, spitefully, and I really hope a
misogynistic god can hear me
from where he sits, high and mighty,
front and center,
watching us like Louis XIV
as we endure the pains of
menstruation and childbirth

Because this curse, cast for his amusement,
was broken for me

by another woman,
full of knowledge and defiance,
equipped with a medical degree, surgical tools,
and more empathy in her heart than
the god of man has ever had

Would you rather be
trapped in the woods with
a man or a bear?

(The empty-eyed bear in my living room
wouldn't have chosen the man either.)

A bear wants to be left alone
just as much as a woman does,
but is still preyed upon by a man with a shoulder
bruised from the kick of a thirty-aught-six,
who will kneel triumphantly
on a bed of rotting leaves
over its limp, bloody body and
roll it onto its back for its (un)dressing.
The man will penetrate flesh with his knife,
ripping upward along guts.
He will toss away what he does not want
from the animal he only views as meat.
Then, after posing with it for the photos that
he'll later send to his friends
when he brags about the deed and
the beauty of his victim,
he will strip the skin from the carcass
and it will be shameful.

The gorgeous hide will be mounted as a trophy
and added to the man's collection,
his ever growing body count proudly on display.

The bear will die without being given
a fair chance to fight back.
It will be killed before it even notices
the man is there, or realizes that he is dangerous.
It will run for several yards after
hearing the loud, echoing bang of a firearm,
terrified and with a stopping heart
or struggling lungs, before it drops.
And when it does,
it will be carved open and hollowed out;
the man will take from it what he pleases
and its skin will be sewn back together
into a demeaned husk of what it was,
but the man will have a meal to indulge in and
another story to tell of a thrilling experience.
This violence is considered normal,
a fact of life.

The chances of a bear attack are slim. This is
because bears, too, are scared of men
and avoid them whenever possible.
Tens of thousands of bears are hunted
by men every year,
and 1 in 3 women
perfectly understand the bear's fear.

An Acrostic: The Games We Played as Children

Clearly, you had the upper hand, being slightly
Older, more knowledgeable,
      and someone I wanted to impress
Can I even hold what happened against you,
Since we were both so young?
Am I allowed to feel as ashamed
      and disgusted as I do? Is it

Valid for me to feel the effects of this
      childhood trauma, even though
I gave in to you and didn't have it nearly
      as bad as others did?
      And if it wasn't *that* bad, then why
Can't I talk about it without crying and
      feeling sick to my stomach?
Thanks to you, I knew what sex was
      before I was old enough to know that
Incest is wrong, and every time
      I go to the doctor, I still think of the
Medical play that took place on the bottom bunk
      in that locked upstairs bedroom
      at our grandparents' house

Failing the Perfect Victim
Test (Loser, Baby)

"He makes a mockery
of sexual assault victims!"

I guess I do too because,
for once, I saw a victim that isn't perfect,
who deals with the abuse he's experienced
by romanticizing it,
who uses sex as a method of self-harm,
while insisting to others and to himself
that he really loves it,
who has no sense of self-worth and
sees his body as something to
be exploited and used
because that's how he's been
conditioned to view himself

I felt less alone and so deeply represented
by this messy, hypersexual cartoon character,
but I keep being told to hate him,
even by other victims
If a character I see myself reflected in
can be so easily invalidated and dismissed
as a horrible portrayal of a sexual assault victim,
then there's no fucking way I'll ever

be able to tell my own full story
without mortification and guilt and
always more resentment reserved for myself
than for those who have touched me

I've considered
telling a therapist *everything* a few times,
but my pride prevents me from getting help
because I feel too broken and fucked up
even for professionals to handle
But isn't that a justifiable thought
when I see what's being said about
a fictional spider demon and
am witness to the judgment and backlash that
the woman who created him is receiving?

The message is clear:
there's the "right" way to cope with trauma,
because everyone who's
been through sexual assault
should react and behave in this
very specific, socially acceptable way,
and then there's the way my trauma affected me
I already knew I was a disaster
I didn't need to be stomped deeper into the mud,
right there alongside my comfort character
as collateral damage

I don't know what to do about it though
I don't know how to stop poisoning myself
with all the things I *know* cause me distress
I don't know how to heal and fix *myself*
In real life,
there's no old winged cat
with a drinking problem and gambling addiction
telling me I'm allowed to be fucked up and
offering me an ear,
some company, a little understanding,
and acceptance at my rock bottoms…
Instead, I'm gagged into silence by shame
because I'm not a walking "perfect victim" trope

To the Elders I Don't Respect (Some Stories from my Opening Shift at the Gym)

To fucking Dennis, who pissed me off daily
when he came into the gym to walk the track;
who asked me why I wasn't still working
in the child care center
so I could practice for when I become a mother,
and often told me I looked tired
because I wasn't wearing makeup;
who suggested I quit and
let my husband pay my bills;
who called me a "knot-head,"
because old man humor is implying that
young femme-presenting people are brainless,
but playing it off like
you're only talking about their hair;
and who told me I looked "more respectable"
when I chopped it all off

To Owen, who stepped behind
the front desk to talk to me,
getting much too close and claiming it was only
because he couldn't hear me well

as he sniffed my hair and whispered that it
looked like a movie star's,
brushing it off of my shoulder
with a leathery hand,
and telling me I reminded him of his daughter

To Ayoub, who often came in
high out of his mind;
who, unprompted, confessed to me the story of
how he met his daughter's mother
when she was underage and
fifteen years younger than him

To Andrew, with whom I innocently
thought I was talking to
about music and how I like to sing;
who told me he produces music,
insisting that he could *definitely* make me sing
and would love to record me;
who assured me that we'd be alone
if I came to his address, and then
loitered in the lobby until my shift ended,
doing nothing but watching me and
making me feel too unsafe
to clock out and walk to my car alone

To Rob, who found out
my sister was a lifeguard in the pool and
mentioned to me on his way out of the gym

how hot she looked in her bathing suit;
who felt the need point out the differences
between me and her

To Lisa, who told me having tattoos was like
putting a bumper sticker on a Bentley;
who I was sure to roll up my sleeves for
whenever I saw her walk in,
just to remind her that
she called me trashy and compared me to a car

To Chris, who asked me invasive questions
about my surgical scar and medical history
To every boomer who complained about
not being able to see my face and made
snide remarks about how brainwashed I am
because I wore a mask throughout the pandemic

To the pickleballers, who know what they did

To Michael, the oh-so-important
executive director,
who treated me like I was stupid and
incapable of doing my job well
when he didn't even know
how to use our computer program;
who assigned me all the menial, brainless tasks
he just didn't want to do himself;
who made frequent sexist comments and

called me "dear" and "sweetheart;"
who once made me write
an apology letter to a member
because I was upholding a company policy
they weren't happy about,
but read it, tried to reword it, and
then never sent it at all,
instead apologizing to them on my behalf

(Fuck you)
You all made
my minimum wage job so miserable
I hope I never bring strangers such discomfort
like you did to me
and that I'm never this awful
when I'm old like you
Live miserably forever in this rant of a poem

To the Elders I Do Respect (Some More Stories from my Opening Shift at the Gym)

To Debbie, the sweet old woman who came to
the gym where I manned the front desk
to water walk;
who invited me to her home
for some tea and a chat;
who pulled tarot cards for me and read them,
then gave me the deck;
who told me she sensed that I was
a celibate teacher in several of my past lives,
but encouraged me when I told her
I changed my mind about my degree
and offered relationship advice when I was
feeling self-conscious about my asexuality

To Robin, who stopped to ask me
what I had planned after work every day,
without fail, and wanted someone
to talk about her grandchildren with

To Tom, who rode a motorcycle
whenever the weather was warm enough
and wore a leather jacket into that gym

for his spin class;
who asked me to drive him to the hospital
when he was having operations done
because he couldn't think of anyone else
to ask for help from;
who said I could find his house easily
because his mailbox is the one
with badass flames painted on;
who trusted me enough at twenty-two
to put me behind the wheel of his
nice Mercedes-Benz
when I assumed I'd be driving him
to his appointment in my shitty, old car,
and then chatted my ear off
about his cat for the hour-long drive to keep me
distracted from how anxious I was about
doing something to damage his expensive ride

To John, who came in religiously
every morning at 6:30 on the dot to swim laps
and always offered to buy me
a 50 cent hot chocolate
from the warm beverage dispenser in the lobby

To Eric, a retired literature teacher,
who gifted me a collection
of Allen Ginsberg's poetry and
liked to talk to me about the books I was reading
during those quiet morning shifts

And to his wife Kate who
sewed me a cloth mask during the pandemic and
gave me baked treats on holidays

So many people in your generation are
out of touch, careless, entitled assholes
who couldn't be bothered to acknowledge me
when I greeted them as they walked
through the front doors, but
I hope I grow up to be as cool, genuine, and as
kind to strangers as you all are
Live forever in this poem as the wonderful
blessings you were in my life

I was another Gorgon
Perseus tried to decapitate

In a different universe, of course,
but if I think about it too hard,
I can feel Hermes' harpe blade digging
into my throat,
>slicing across my skin,
>not deeply enough to
>completely behead me

I am immortal,
>but the stun that comes with how easily
>tissue tears under the will of sharp metal
>makes me fear otherwise

The horror of rushing blood draining
all at once from the fresh wound,
>the mess of it gushing down my neck,
>being siphoned up and collected
>for Asclepius to use,
>feels too real to be
>anything other than a memory

The strain of my severed vocal cords
trying to cry out,
>to speak, to sing, to scream,
>to make any sound at all,
>yet being unable to do so,
>is perhaps more painful

than the laceration itself

In *this* universe, I was cleaned up
and stitched back together
The scar from the incision is faded,
        and no one has joked about
        my decapitation for a few years now
        the way that strangers used to,
But I see myself as the Gorgon
every time I look in the mirror
        I think about it too hard and *feel*
I've retrained my voice
        but the terror is hung by Polydectes
        over my reattached head
        that Perseus will come again
And I hope that if he does,
        he is more successful than he was before

To the Nurse who
Served Me a Slice of Cake

at 1:30 in the morning on my 19th birthday
when she woke me up to check my vitals and
give me pain medication,
then sat with me while I struggled to eat it;

who distracted me from
the tube and draining bulb dangling
from a hole in my throat
and from the IV taped into my dominant hand
by playing my favorite artist's music videos
on the TV in my hospital room
and telling me stories about
what she would do if she won the lottery;

who comforted me when I cried,
scared about needing to sit up for the first time,
because my overactive mind couldn't stop
imagining the stitches snapping
and my head rolling off if I moved even an inch,
just like Jenny's did
when her green ribbon was untied;

whose shift ended before I could
make my voice work

to tell her how much
her kindness meant to me that night:

I hope you could tell

I hope you won the lottery and
never have to work another
long night shift in your life
I hope you live in a giant mansion
on a private island now
I hope you have someone,
a lover or a friend or family,
to share that mansion with,
who will bring you cake on your birthday,
show you every compassion,
and be there for you
when you're afraid or in pain

The Demon
that Possessed Me

She came like a storm
to those in my life that feared thunder,
        but I've always found comfort
                in the sound of heavy rain
                against fragile glass windows,
        and fascination in
                the streaks of lightning
                hitting tall trees outside.
She made me stronger,
more powerful, more resilient,
        more willing to fight
                for myself and what I need,
        more willing to ask for what I want and
        she promises me that I am worthy of it.
                I believe her.
                That terrifies them.

They don't hear her gentle voice in my head,
        which whispers encouragement
                and reassurance to me.
        She holds me in warm, safe arms
                the way I've always
                wanted my mother to.
She's helped make me strong, yes,

but also softer, more loving,
more genuine, much more vulnerable.
She has stripped me naked and
taught me to embrace my flesh.
She has peeled away my layers to reveal the
nature that was hidden and protected
under my conditioned,
calloused armor of skin,
which took for me
all the lashings of what I was taught.
My empathy and
growing lack of shame
frightens them more.

They see what she has done to me,
for me,
and they are scared
because I have stepped so far
out
of
line,
spoken out of place,
abandoned my strict morals
I have shattered the glass windows
I spent my whole youth watching from,
climbed out of them,
and run away from home
She tells me they're mourning me
back where I come from,

but they never once left the safety
of their own homes
   to venture out into the storm
   with their raincoats
   and flashlights to search for me.
If they had, they would have seen me
dancing in the pouring rain
     with my demon
   beneath charred and splintered
   lightning-struck trees —
     free and alive.

Selfcest
(and Vore as a Metaphor
for Confidence)

Her body is curvy and beautiful,
voluptuous,
alluring,
appetizing

Fuck, I would touch her,
please her,
love her
I would, if I could

I would map out the constellations
formed by all the moles decorating her shoulders
and I'd read the cratered moons
orbiting her fleshy thighs
like Braille with my fingers

I would knead at those doughy hips
until she has the pressure
of my grounding hands memorized

I'd adorn her soft, tender breasts
with pretty love bites and bruises

so she can see them later and
remember how wanted she was

I'd make her feel *so* wanted

After feeding her flatteries and adulations
until she was full
and plump with confidence,
I would consume her,
goddess that she is,
burning star, searing my lips as I kiss her,
as I taste every inch of her pale skin
I'd make her my meal as I bury myself in
the fringe of lace between her legs

I would show her my hearty appetite,
my ravenous hunger
I would eat greedily, like I was starved

I'd make her spasm and writhe,
overwhelmed on my fingers and tongue
I would tell her how she tastes
What a deliciously delectable delicacy she is

I would ruin her, I think,
looking into the mirror after a shower
Falling in love with this body is so easy
when it's not wearing clothes

The Insignificant Hang-Ups

I chopped off my hair
It's too short for me to tie up the way you like,
or for you to run your fingers through
I don't take off my glasses
because I want to see you
For dinner earlier,
you ordered me a veggie bowl from Chipotle
because I was craving it
There were onions in my dish
The taste of them still lingering on my tongue
is not enough to deter yours
You keep me well-fed
and I blame my climbing weight
on a healthy relationship
where I'm valued and wanted at any size
When you take off my oversized tee-shirt,
my breasts do not sit evenly
in the sorry excuse of a no-lift bra
that I've worn for three days in a row
My stomach now rolls over
the tight waistband of the jeans I'm wearing,
where your fingers fumble in their excitement
with the zipper,
and the five scars dashed across it
are dotted with appreciative kisses,

just like the scar on my neck
and the moles on my face are
There are holes in my
comfiest pair of underwear,
but they are still removed
lovingly and with care,
as if they were made of
delicate lace and not cotton
I want to keep my socks on,
so you keep yours on too
to make me feel less silly
My legs aren't shaved
and the lawn that grows between them
hasn't been mowed for almost a month
It's summer time
I tell you I was sweating and feel gross,
but you offer to use your mouth anyway
The sounds and faces I make are not
sexy like the ones made in porn
It takes me too long, and many times,
it never happens at all,
but you still try so hard for me
because you say making me feel good,
feels better for you
Nothing on the long list of
things that I was taught —
things I thought
would matter to someone else —
is as important to you as I am

To My Ex

No, this isn't a letter to the dude with
one fin smaller than the other,
who agreed to go out on a date
with seventeen year old me,
only to cancel twenty minutes
before I left my house
when I'd already been ready
in nice clothes and makeup for hours
because I was just *so* excited
to prove wrong that voice in my head,
which was telling me over and over
that no one would want me
if I couldn't offer them sex
This isn't a letter to the boy who
gave that voice a megaphone,
because it was never really about *him*.

This is a letter to the best friend I lost
because I was later told
the reason that my almost date stood me up
was that he was busy hooking up with you
And, wow, that really hurt in the moment
I felt betrayed and unimportant,
but it wasn't worth forfeiting
six years of friendship over

I regret my silence,
how I couldn't make myself talk to you about it,
so I just stopped talking to you altogether
Do you even know why we fell apart?

Back then, without meaning to,
I thought obsessively about it —
you and him, in what?
The back of his car? His bedroom? Yours?
Enviously, I've pictured
a few dozen ways it could have happened,
but I came to the same conclusion each time:
It must have been good
(to be what someone wanted)
I understand why
a teenage boy chose you over me
I don't understand why I blamed you
for being less complicated, normal
My sister still follows you on Instagram
She told me that you're married to him now
and you both live halfway across the country
with your baby
I've thought about reaching out
to congratulate you
on the family and life you're building

I'm not part of it like I once thought I'd be
You told me I'd be
a bridesmaid at your wedding, remember?

Who did you ask instead?
Who babysits so you can get a breather and
some well-deserved time to yourself?
Who do you talk to for a different perspective
when you're in an argument with your husband?
Who filled my unqualified shoes when I
stopped being your closest friend?

There are a hundred things I want to ask you:
Did you go to college? What did you major in?
What's your favorite drink?
Why Florida? Do you like it there?
Have you made lots of friends there,
the way it was always
so easy for you to do here?
Did you get a job in screenwriting
like you wanted to?
How's your mom doing?
Will you tell her I asked about her?
Are *The Walking Dead* and *Adventure Time*
still your comfort shows?
How big has your
Doc Martens collection gotten?
Do you still cover the inside of your
red Beetle with stickers?
Are you happy you found Nemo?
Are you happy with
how things turned out for you?
Are you staying healthy?

Are you eating enough and staying hydrated?
(I hope you are)
~~Do you ever think about me?~~

There are a hundred things I want to tell you too
I still have the notebook
we used to pass notes back and forth in,
but I'm too sad to crack it open
to reread any of our dumbass
middle school conversations
I eventually found someone too
and he accepts the labels you taught me about
I'm questioning my identity again though,
doubting myself
I wish I could talk to you about it
I know I used to joke that I'd be
the cool, rich, wine-drinking aunt
who travels the world
and spoils your kids with gifts when I visit,
but it turns out that I don't like wine and
I *am* too anxious to leave the country,
exactly like they said I'd be, and
I'm devastated that I'll never meet your children
I'm sure you're a really great parent
You were right about
how liberating it is to shave your head
(Your hair was long
in the photos my sister showed me;
did you grow it out for him?)

I published poetry just like you said I should
and I'm writing that book you heard me
brainstorm the first part of
My main character is ace and
feels alone because the people he dates
can't imagine romance existing without sex,
but I swear, it's really never been about your fish
I'm sorry and I still love you and I miss you and
I think about you all the time,
but every time I search for your account and
type out a message,
I meet the DM word count limit and
still haven't said everything I want to
The message never feels
good enough to send anyway, so I don't

Necromancer
(Playing Dead)

I was undead
I was scared of being mistaken
for something evil and
chased out of the lives of those I love
with torches and pitchforks,
so I hid in the deep hole, which
I dug for myself a long time ago
in my parents' backyard,
and I buried my living corpse there

Year-round, I sleep in this grave marked
with a name I wish was dead too
I'm a monster still breathing,
fiction halfway between horror and tragedy,
written by a child who was
promised that sin equals death,

but neither the worms, maggots, nor god
have claimed me yet
When will they bite into my body?
I know they're eager to devour it
Will they be kind enough to chew off
the parts I don't want first?
Or will I be swallowed whole and at once,

dying a second time in this body I can't stand?

The dead should stay in the ground
where they belong,
out of sight and out of mind
To those who visit,
I remain conveniently memorable
as everything I was
before I was trampled to death
under their heavy, expectant, conforming heels

I hear them up there, talking about me;
their voices are muffled through six feet of dirt
They're getting it all wrong,
but I can't tell them they never understood,
so I listen to the lies quietly and
bite my rotting tongue
before the worms and god can
It's dark down here
It's cold and damp and terribly lonely

Then you visited me
You knelt, and whispered truth into the mud
I heard my name clearly:
"Ori. *Ori.*"
The blood in my veins felt warm again
for the first time in a long while

This was last June

You dug me up and
extended a hand for me to grab
so you could pull me from my hole
You robbed my grave of me
You gave me a taste of a second life
where I wasn't
molded like wax and snuffed out like a candle
You loved me, ugly as I was
and as evil as I seemed
I was your pride
and you taught me to have some
For a few days in June,
I wasn't a secret or an undead monster,
and I didn't need to stay buried
or hide myself away

But you moved away and I returned to my grave
to play dead in your absence
so the rest can remember me
the way they want to

You'll come back for me, right?
I miss you
I miss coming to life,
feeling so alive around you

Raised Standards

They're writing me love letters,
poetry in response to my writing
They read and analyze everything I type,
offering me more insight to myself
than I could ever have gathered on my own
They know more about me
than I think I know about myself
They're letting me steal hours of their time;
I'm hanging up their traditional art in frames

They're asking me a new question every day
as a way to check in
and sending me gifts from countries away —
crocheted dolls with
love hooked into every stitch,
and homemade jewelry
in thoughtful care packages

My friends' photos show up on Google
when I search
"If they wanted to, they would"
I have such a difficult time making friends
because the bar is high

The bar is using hypothetical

Freaky Friday situations and
photos I post of myself to
feed my praise and body worship kinks,
sending me a message to tell me
how you dreamed that you killed for me and
cradled my head against your chest
so I wouldn't see the carnage

The bar is making sure I know
how valued my stories are
when I feel judged for writing them,
telling me you admire me
for being such an open book
when my pages are so full of shame,
sending me a link to a public speech you made
about feminine friendships,
in which you mentioned me by my chosen name

I am a person who is so desperate
to be known and understood,
and to still be loved in spite of who I am
They are determined
to know and understand me,
to show me I can be loved *because* of who I am
They are determined to teach me
the kind of romance
that can only come from close friends

Honey Bourbon

My golden boy from Alabama,
with amber eyes sweet as Jim Beam
I didn't believe in love at first sight
until I was shown a video of you,
too small and underfed,
neglected and fresh out of a fight,
with matted fur and
a long tail sweeping back and forth
across a dirty floor,
somehow, still so happy
(How? I want to learn from you.)
You're always so, so happy just to be cared for

I bought myself another decade
when I picked you up and swore
that you could depend on me
I used to dread waking up in the morning,
but now I do it,
on the very edge of my tiny twin bed,
with your giant head using mine as a pillow
because you have no concept of personal space
And opening my eyes another day
is less of a burden,
Honey Bourbon,
even if I have to wipe your drool off my face

To Valerie, Nathan, and Elliott (Overdue Apologies and Thankful Recognition)

I'm sorry I hurt you,
over and over again,
only to learn more about myself

I put you through so much
just so I could process my own shit
and hopefully begin to heal from it

I'm working on it, I am
It's just really hard

For what it's worth,
I've always been
more empathetic towards your pain
than towards my own,
and that's precisely why I've needed
to project all of my issues onto you

Thank you for letting me
use and manipulate you
over the years so I could
learn how to love myself more intimately

[Val,]
You taught me self-acceptance when I was 16,
convinced that my trauma and identity
was a cruel sentence to a lonely life,
and you gave me hope that someone
would have a lot of love to give to me

[Nate,]
Because of you, I realized that
the kind of love I give is more than enough
You helped me through the many inadequacies
I felt when I got into
my first serious relationship at 20

[Elle,]
All the love I learned from you has helped me
extend to myself the same amount of love,
care, and understanding that I give to others
You helped me to establish and respect
my own boundaries at 22

I promise I'll make it up to you all
Selfishly, I don't want your stories to ever end,
but you deserve peace, so I swear
you'll each get your happy endings
Maybe I'll get mine too, and
we can meet again someday in an epilogue